SAINT JEANNIE'S SHINY BLACK SHOES

Achieving Holiness in Secular Times: A Pragmatic Example to Follow

Farewell reminiscences by Jeannie Hughes
compiled with commentaries by her
husband, Al

SAINT JEANNIE'S SHINY BLACK SHOES
Achieving Holiness in Secular Times: A Pragmatic Example to Follow
by
Gloria Jean Hughes and Albert E. Hughes

Designed by James Kent Ridley

Published by Goodbooks Media

Printed in the United States of America

Ad Majorem Dei Gloriam

ISBN-13: 978-1517502850

ISBN-10: 1517502853

GOODBOOKS MEDIA

3453 Aransas
Corpus Christi, Texas, 78411
goodbooksmedia.com

FOR
Shannon, Katie and Martha

IN THANKSGIVING
for the Love Justice and Mercy of our Triune
God

DEDICATION
To all who live the High Calling

ACKNOWLEDGMENT

Many there are whose lives influenced Jeannie's pursuit of life in the Spirit over the last thirty seven years, from her Pentecostal encounter of the Holy Spirit in 1978 until her death this July. Most notable among them should be mentioned the priests, deacons and laity active in the many charismatic communities allied with the Southern California Renewal Conference (SCRC) and the Benedictine monks of The Monastery of the Risen Christ in San Luis Obispo, CA. Their Spiritual Directors School was a vital source of understanding.

Nor can we omit mention of Father S. James Farfaglia, our pastor, friend and spiritual guide of these last dozen years.

As to this little book, our good friend and publisher, James Ridley, has done it again, turning an unadorned manuscript into a thing of beauty.

Most of all we give thanks and acknowledgment to God, who revealed His presence to Jeannie, accepted her vows of obedience, and led her to greater heights.

Albert E. Hughes, Lt Col, USAF (retired), M.S., M.M., Oblate, OSB
corneliuscenturion@gmail.com

INTRODUCTION

There are people who teach neither by lecture, nor debate, nor by Socratic questioning, but by the conduct of their life. Jeannie was one such. Orphaned before her teens, from out of her loss of parental love and the intense loneliness of a child moved about, there came a new measure of love and care for the sufferings of others that is seldom seen. Such is the stuff of holiness. From such does a wounded healer emerge. Accomplished in league with Sacramental life, a holy Saint may be found. But a caution….

Exclusive of the exhaustive deliberations of the Roman Catholic Church, and perhaps as well that of the eastern orthodox churches; no mortal definitively may speak to the final destination of another's soul. So you will not read here in any definitive way of Jeannie as being in Heaven. That would be the modern understanding of the word "saint." One who is definitively, authoritatively (canonically) declared to be "in Heaven." But in the first century sense of the word; a saint is one who authentically follows Jesus, *Christos*, in the sacramental life of His Universal (Catholic) Church.

Our purpose is to demonstrate through testimony that Gloria Jean "Jeannie" McCaffery Hughes, by her sacramental life of selfless devotion, is qualified, for – in Saint Paul's words – *the crown of justice,* that her adult life is a practical example that others may follow in their quest of the holy life. In the gospels it is written: *One who would be the greatest in the kingdom, shall be the servant of all.* These words, scripturally attributed to *Christos*, are the basis for our demonstration of practical holiness by the life of Jeannie in this secular age of rampant apostasy.

Our primary source is the testimony of Jeannie, herself. As she first sensed the early sting of an onrushing Alzheimer's death, she wrote her own life testimony. It is a simple statement intended for the edification of her siblings and her children. No other intent of hers is known. It was sincere, heartfelt, and had the urgency of one who is making a last attempt to share Faith with those she loved: her spouse, siblings and children. Her personal testimony has not been altered in any way.

The second source is testimony of the author, a witness of Jeannie's life as friend and husband for 48 years; providing a commentary that fills in other observations and facts for the benefit of a more general audience beyond that which Jeannie originally intended.

The last source is her eulogy given at the rosary, the evening before Mass and burial. The eulogy fills in other blanks for a general audience and provides a repeated transition from stage to stage of Jeannie's maturing quest of holy life as her spiritual awakening progressed. Her's is a text book case for study by those who would follow *Christos* in our times.

Gloria Jean Hughes,
Servant of All
December 17, 1945 - July 25, 2015

"She'd say something profound, almost off-handedly,
and even follow with a laugh — her special Jeannie
laugh — to soften, but not contradict the truth of what
she said. She really did have her unique style."

Linda Wade Williams

JEANNIE'S TESTIMONY:
CHILDHOOD

If I really wanted to feel sorry for myself, I could look back on my life as a series of painful events, but when I was about 32 years old I had a very deep spiritual awakening. When I do look back on my life, I see that the Lord is very much a part in those events and there is a purpose in all that happens to me. I am just sorry that I did not see his hand in it all at the time. I always was sure in the early days that I was making all the difficult decisions on my own.

My mother died when I was about eight years old. I was attending Holy Rosary Catholic School at the time, and the nuns very much loved my mother. At her death, the nuns took very special care of my brother Skip and I. (I was told years later that my mother had cooked at the convent, probably before I was born.)

The church was across the street from the school and in those days, if we were near the church grounds before school we were expected to attend Mass. We also could make visits during the lunch hour if we wanted. I did find myself there often after my mother died; lighting candles at the large statue of Mary holding Christ, her son, on her lap after the Crucifixion.

The nuns told us in the first grade, and probably in the second as we prepared for First Holy Communion, that the prayers we said when we lighted the candles went straight to Heaven – faster than without the candles. I lighted a lot of candles. I knew God could bring my mother back if he wanted to. I painfully was aware that I was the only one among my friends without a mother. Well, that prayer faded sometimes after I turned twelve, but I always found myself in a church somewhere when I felt troubled.

My older brother Skip and I (I was the youngest child) lived with our father for a couple of years. Dad then was committed to a mental hospital after a mental breakdown. Skip and I then moved in with Mickey, our oldest brother, for about a year. He had been married just two or three years at the time, and they had a baby boy. It was a difficult situation for all of us.

My father died when I was fourteen. I have fond memories of him with his wonderful sense of fun. He took us fishing and to the park in Seattle. We did not have much money, but he let me choose my own clothes as far back as I can remember. And I remember his great smile when he surprised me with a little present.

My oldest sister, Bernice, about 20 at the time, knew a case worker with Catholic Charities; I was asked if I wanted to try living in a foster home. I made that difficult decision at age twelve, staying with Ed and Marilyn Bond until age nineteen.

COMMENT: Much has been written about the psychological devastation visited upon the young by the loss of a parent. In West Seattle, the children of Joseph and Alice McCaffery were visited with this devastation twice; first the mother who died young of cancer; soon thereafter the father, who developed acute paranoia, was institutionalized and died of a heart attack. All this in the most critical years for development of young children and early teens.

The worst impact fell to Jeannie and her closest brother, who were unprepared, too young to handle their losses as transitioning young adults. Particularly, Jeannie lamented throughout her life over the loss of her mother. It is painful to read this part of her testimony, more painful to read it having shared in her periodic lamentations throughout her adult life. Memory of her lost mother haunted Jeannie; a memory kept alive by framed pictures of Alice still found throughout our house; a beautiful young woman cut short in time. It also is clear from all that Jeannie remembered, that Alice was full of love for all her children, but may have doted particularly on little Jeannie, knowing that she, Alice, soon would die. Perhaps in the short time she had, Alice wanted to imprint her love as a basis of Jeannie's own life of love. If so, it certainly worked as you will see.

But something else also was going on, begun in those early years. Jeannie only was told this in her sixties, after her diagnosis of Alzheimer's. As teens, the older three siblings had concluded that Jeannie was responsible for their mother's death. While carrying Jeannie, Alice deferred cancer treatment until Jeannie was born. Alice appears to have given her life in exchange for Jeannie's, according to the model of Saint Gianna Molla.

It would appear their assignment of fault, oft repeated in juvenile minds, sank into a paradigmatic family assumption, perhaps unrecognized, but influencing their behavior toward Jeannie. In short, she, with our children, often were ostracized, ignored by Jeannie's elder siblings. That caused Jeannie additional pangs of sorrow, born of love, for many years.

Yet, there is no cause for assignment of blame. They all were young, then, and all suffered the loss of parents and the psychological pains-beyond-understanding that were to follow.

JEANNIE'S TESTIMONY:
A TIME TO BE FOSTERED

My foster parents wanted to adopt me, but I had my own siblings still in my life and I felt a great sense of loyalty to my dead parents. I also liked my own last name better. I must have had a great sense of identity, but whatever the reason, I know I did not want to be adopted.

(l. to r.) three teen foster girls (Jeannie's face showing),
Marilyn Bond, Panama Canal boat pilot.

Ed Bond was a Boeing engineer with a great love of boating. He designed and built a 45 foot cruising catamaran in the back yard.

Con Amour Ashore

I got to choose the colors (two tone pink and salmon!) and Ed taught me how to paint the boat.

As we were finishing the boat, Boeing transferred Ed from Seattle to New Orleans. We sailed that boat down the coast, through the Panama Canal and back up to New Orleans where we lived aboard and survived a hurricane at the dock on Lake Pontchartrain.

After a year, I was nineteen, I flew back to Seattle and worked for Travelers Insurance. While at Seattle, Ed was transferred again, this time to Cape Canaveral to work on the Apollo program. Soon, I was invited to join them, but mightily resisted until a three month Seattle monsoon softened me up. Ed was planning a sail to the Caribbean in the summer of 1967, so I flew down to live with them on the boat, without a clue as to what was about to happen.

———————◆◆◆———————

COMMENT: A sense of identity? Rock solid. I do not remember ever seeing her step out of who she was as a moral, faithful, Catholic woman, to put on a persona of someone else! Her identity extended not only to her name (which she gave up only through sacramental marriage) but to her ideals, her will, her integrity and her resistance to anyone who would try to change her – including me!

The catamaran was named *Con Amour*, "with love." Perhaps prophetic. Jeannie didn't just "get to choose the colors," it was a deal. Ed wanted her to share the work by painting the boat – two 45 foot hulls with a deck to keel sheer of about nine feet, both decks over the hulls, the wing deck between them and the cabin above that, which doubled as the dining and sitting room. A huge project. She accepted only on the condition that she chose the colors. Ed capitulated and the boat was painted two tone pink and salmon! In all our days under sail, I never saw another boat of any kind painted like that. (Interesting it is, that salmon, besides being Jeannie's favorite color at the time, is the traditional color of peace!)

If you can find a copy, the boat's construction and first voyage is documented as chapter 11 of *The International Book of Catamarans and Trimarans* by Edward F. Cotter, Captain, USCG, copyright 1966. And no, you can't have my copy. They are too hard to find, these days.

Departing Seattle

That sail to New Orleans was no small matter, either. Jeannie never had been on an all-up, in the water, operating sail boat of any kind. Her first sailing experience was out Puget Sound, down the coast of Washington, Oregon, California, Mexico, and Central America, through the Panama Canal, up through a Gulf storm that stranded them at Swan Island for three days, and on to the Mississippi River and New Orleans. As you might imagine, she learned to sail the hard way in seas that reached 50 feet in wave height at times. They even suffered a knock down off the coast of Mexico, mast in the water! Ed designed her well. *Con Amour* righted herself and the voyage continued with a water salted crew and two really irritated cats!

Con Amour's first passage

JEANNIE'S TESTIMONY: COURTSHIP

There was a young Air Force Captain living on a sailboat in the adjacent dock. We married at the end of September, that year. I was twenty one, he twenty six.

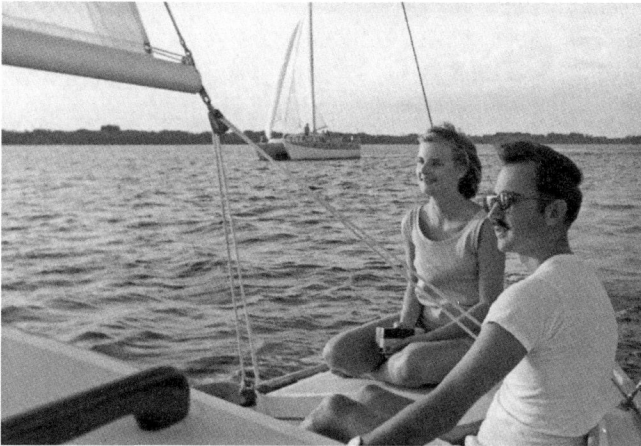

Courtship. *Con Amour*, Ship of Chaperone, following

It was most improbable: as a teen, Ed had warned me not to marry an engineer, a military man, or a non-Catholic. Al Hughes was all three! When he was a teen, he had been warned by his father, "Never marry a Catholic, and it would be best if you never dated one."

Both sets of parents witnessed our marriage! We both often are amused when we recall the circumstances.

(That summer, before the marriage. we made the trip to the Caribbean: eight people aboard a 45 foot sailboat for six weeks. If ever a planned relationship could be tested, that was it. We battled bad weather, bad tempers, bad smells, tight quarters, and all of us battled sea sickness at one time or another, except Al. There was no hiding bad habits! It was a concentrated courtship in the presence of my foster parents and high seas! Returning to Florida, we all agreed that the proposed marriage likely would last.)

—————◆—————

COMMENT: A young Air Force Captain, I was working nearby at Patrick AFB, the home base of the Air Force Eastern Test Range. It was during the Apollo moon landing program, the 1960's, and I was managing the development of special purpose Doppler radars. In those days the technology and accuracy of such radars were classified secrets, but now, every weather station seems to have one. We were tracking the precise motion of missiles and space boosters after launch; today they are tracking rain drops and wind driven debris.

My plan was an Air Force career and eternal bachelorhood. However, Ed and Marilyn had their own plan and three foster daughters back in Seattle. After Ed and Marilyn got to know me (we were next door dock-neighbors) foster daughter number one showed up. I was polite, but disinterested. After a few weeks, she went back to Seattle. Soon, foster daughter number two showed up. Now I was suspicious, but polite and disinterested. Did not date that one either. In due time she left, to my relief.

But then Marilyn started saying, "Jeannie is coming to visit. You'll *like* Jeannie!" Now there was no doubt; suspicions confirmed! On the immediate weekend I arranged for a dock space in another town. I was to move the following weekend.

Jeannie arrived on that Tuesday, late in March. Promptly, I was invited to dinner on the *Con Amour*. Apparently, Jeannie knew of the plan, too, because we glared at each other when I stepped aboard. Still, with the move scheduled for Saturday, I had not arranged for a weekend date. On Friday after work, with nothing left to do before the move, I invited Jeannie to go out. We wound up at a nightclub with booths, a small dance floor and a noisy local band. After our first dance, we returned to sip our drinks. I offered a second dance; she said "No." I said, "Good!" It turned out that neither of us liked to dance. We started talking, a conversation that lasted 48 years.

And how did that sail to the Caribbean test our proposed marriage? Ten days in close quarters with four to eight people living within 45 feet of one another on a hard beat from the coast of Florida to San Juan, that's how. If you are not familiar with sailing, especially ocean sailing, let me explain. In sailing parlance, to *beat* is to sail opposite (into) the wind at an angle off the wind direction of around 45 degrees, maybe a little closer, but not much. That also means you are sailing against the general direction of the waves. Doesn't mean much in one foot seas, but try that in four or five or more feet of onrushing waves. Plowing into four or five foot waves at sailing speed. with repeated salt water showers and inches of water running across the deck, can be fun for a few hours, like a pillow fight with hard pillows, but try doing that for ten days, 24/7, in close quarters as we did. "Aye, matey, it can try the soul!" And we did, together, just fine.

JEANNIE'S TESTIMONY:
EARLY MARRIED LIFE

A t our wedding Mass, Fr Power related the story of Ruth and emphasized to me that I was called to show that same faithfulness as Ruth; willing to go wherever my husband was called; he was in the Air Force. Many times over the years I have recalled those words, picked up our belongings and followed my husband, though I often was unsure of Al's chosen assignments. Every time was an occasion

A most unlikely wedding

of personal growth. The places I resisted held particularly special and joyful surprises for me.

When Al requested assignment to the Space Defense Center in Colorado, we knew he would have to go remote the following year. He volunteered for and transferred to Clear Air Force Station in central Alaska. He volunteered for that assignment because it was the only one where the family could stay nearby – in Fairbanks! We drove up to, and back a year later from, Alaska. During

Jeannie with Shannon; Fairbanks, AK

his breaks, he carpooled or train-pooled to Fairbanks, so that we hardly were separated at all! It was in Fairbanks that I miscarried at a very early term. I named him Kevin. His memory is always with me.

All together we moved nine times in sixteen years with the Air Force and thrice since then. But the greatest of all was our two year tour on the island of Antigua, West Indies. With two little daughters in the house, three and a half year old Shannon and infant Katie, mightily I had resisted the move to Antigua, but once in place many blessings of personal growth occurred.

COMMENT: "…faithfulness as Ruth…" The day before the wedding, Ed, at dockside, asked me to take on a nuanced commitment in addition to the traditional vows. He said that Jeannie was a special person, fragile in health and – he did not use the word "holy," (then agnostic, I would not have understood) – and of great innocence; religious and moral integrity. He wanted extra assurance that I would protect her always and without fail. I readily committed myself to that end.

Soon after marriage Jeannie and I made another commitment. Regardless of USAF duties, we would do our best never to be separated, one from another. Jeannie requested this, probably out of her fear of feeling helpless and alone as she did so often in her childhood. Even at Fairbanks, we held to that commitment.

Fear of the unknown always seems stronger than fear of the known. In the days leading up to the Antiguan assignment, Jeannie was beside herself with fear. She knew all too well the protocol responsibility that was about to descend on her shoulders, and she already felt fully occupied with responsibility for our two baby girls. She went so far as to wish, in my hearing, that a volcano would blow up the island so that we could not go. (Not seriously, of course, but a measure of her concern.)

JEANNIE'S TESTIMONY:
CARIBBEAN LIFE

A I was the commander of Antigua Air Station, with duties that included high level diplomatic work with several governments: Antigua, Great Brittan, Canada and Venezuela. We counted US ambassadors, consular officials, generals, and admirals;

Jeannie and author. Shoulder to shoulder, always.

British colonial island governors, premiers and ministers with varied portfolios among our frequent house guests. Many became friends and of course, the protocol duties in countless social situations fell to me. We even were presented to Queen Elizabeth II on one occasion!

Sir Luther (center left looking at camera) and Lady Winter (rear center wearing sunglasses)

———————— ≋ ————————

COMMENT FROM HER EULOGY: I first began to understand the servanthood of Jeannie during our sojourn in the Caribbean. For two years there, our home received a constant parade of notables. I remember Air Force General Parks and General Marshall; various British brigadiers, ship captains and admirals; several knights of the British realm, Doctor Sir Luther and Lady Winter and Governor, Sir Wilfred and Lady Jacobs among them. I remember Premier Vere Bird and his various ministers with and without portfolio, British government representative Ian and Mrs. Thow; and several US ambassadors: including Ortiz, assigned at Barbados, and Sally from D.C. For all of these notables and more, (most usually at our cocktail parties ,but also overnight visitors as house guests), Jeannie was the gracious hostess; filled with the same charm, grace, humility, peace, charity, loving kindness and solicitude all our friends and acquaintances have come to know in these last years. She truly was the servant of all. But, there is more.

There also were our half blind, elderly gardener; our maid Dorsett Lincoln; a variety of Antiguan bartenders working our cocktail parties; a host of junior officers off of British warships, and fishermen who brought lobster to our kitchen door. All these also were party to the same charm, grace, humility, peace, charity, loving kindness and solicitude received by the notables and by all who have come to know Jeannie in these last years. She truly was the servant of all. But there is more.

The children. O, the island children. Jeannie's jitney became famous in the Northwest quadrant of the island. In her drives down to the capital, St. John's, she would encounter many native children walking to and from town or school who, from roadside, would sing out "Mrs. Hughes, a ride, a ride please!" There was always room for one more. She often arrived in town with our car crammed full of chattering, laughing, singing native children. All these, of more humble station, were party to the same charm grace, humility, peace, charity, loving kindness and solicitude received by all who have come to know Jeannie in these last years. She truly was the servant of all.

It was early in October, 1977, that my mother reminded me of a passage in the Old Testament.

"The just will stand before kings." And so it was that in the late evening of 28 October 1977 on the promenade deck aboard Her Majesty's Yacht *Britannia*, Jeannie stood toe to toe with Her Most Excellent Majesty Elizabeth II, Queen of England. Jeannie with the same charm, grace, humility, peace, charity, loving kindness and solicitude known to all who have come to know her in these last years. She truly was the servant of all. But there is more.

HMY Britannia

JEANNIE'S TESTIMONY: LIFE IN THE SPIRIT

Best of all, during those two years Al had multiple encounters with the Lord, converted from agnosticism to Catholicism, and both of us encountered the Holy Spirit in a clear and profound Pentecostal (Charismatic) experience. That was to change our lives completely since we then vowed unconditional obedience to God. We soon learned that He took our vow most seriously. When a family turns its life over to the Lord and says "Thy will be done", life can be like getting on a roller coaster: lots of peaks and valleys. But there is no turning back; trust and go.

Pentecost; Acts 2:1-4

Because we moved so frequently, and perhaps because I grew up without my natural mother, I had chosen with the first childbirth to stay at home and concentrate on the welfare of my children, on Christian family life. From that time forward, I also chose volunteer work that would not interfere with the children. As they grew older, they participated with us in many church projects. Returning to Patrick AFB, Florida for the last time, we formed the on base youth group with another couple. The girls always went with us on outings. That was our first sense of church community, working together in small groups.

Then came the big surprise. The Lord asked Al to retire from the USAF! That was probably the hardest decision Al ever made. After a short delay, Al obeyed, contrary to his own will. No job prospects, no clue as to what would come next; but trust and wait. The answer came a couple of months later in a little add I found in a church newspaper: an invitation to apply for a Master of Pastoral Ministry at Seattle University. Al applied, and in June, 1983 we were on our way.

We were there for a year. During that time I focused on the family, but also worked with street children down town, providing food and just showing our concern for them as best we could. After one year, the next move was to Santa Maria, CA. Al found a job on a civilian contract at Vandenberg AFB doing what he had done the last few years in the Air Force.

(All of these moves since Antigua and the last one yet to come were accompanied by Spiritual indications and confirming miracles. The story is told in Al's PARADISE COMMANDER, published by Goodbooks Media

COMMENT: There are many Theological and Philosophical *deductive* arguments for the existence of a spiritual, unseen realm and for a Transcendent Other which we call God. In the current state of *inductively* reasoned science, even Astrophysicists are now declaring overwhelming statistical proof, that undeniably there must be a universe-designing and universe-sustaining, transcendent Creator. (Read *New Proofs for the Existence of God*, by Robert J. Spitzer.)

Nevertheless, the reality of the Transcendent Other, whom we call God, is best discovered by personal experience. Experience also reveals that dialog of a sort is available with the Transcendent, under conditions well known to serious religious persons. (Read *Paradise Commander*, mentioned just above, for examples. Also, read *Acts of the*

Apostles, Chapter 2, regarding Pentecost as an example of an encounter with the Holy Spirit.)

COMMENT FROM HER EULOGY: The years fly by. In Seattle, you could find Jeannie downtown on street corners, serving meals, solicitude and consolation to abandoned street kids with the same charm, grace, humility, peace, charity, loving kindness and solicitude many have come to know of her in these last years. She truly was the servant of all. But there is more.

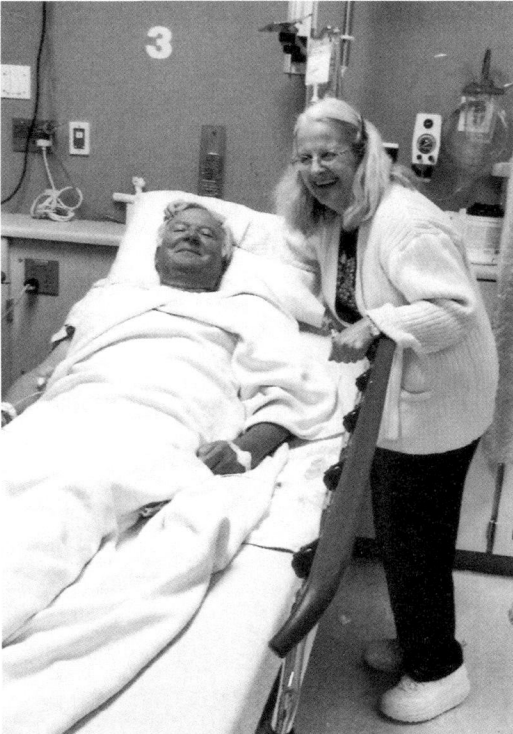

JEANNIE'S TESTIMONY:
CALIFORNA LIFE

In Santa Maria my children grew up and I found more volunteer work with teens in the detention center, visiting on Sunday and Thursday. With a priest we held mass on Sunday for them all, though many were not Catholic. The visits were amazing to me; kids discover they need God when they get in deep trouble. It gave me great pleasure to be with them, remembering my youthful need of God when troubled. On Thursdays we met in visiting rooms to talk about spiritual matters. Sometimes we were their only visitors. Families had turned their back on their own. We gave them a time to see that someone cared for them without judgment. I also was the unofficial "librarian" at the Josephite seminary.

And there was the RCIA. Al's practicum at Seattle U. was the RCIA. We founded and he directed the RCIA program at St Louis de Montfort for many years. Once again, I was the protocol "officer", group leader, etc, etc. etc. My focus was hospitality as we quickly learned that people inquiring about the Catholic faith also usually are looking for community. I wanted to make sure people felt warmth and welcome when they came to our meetings.

In my home I facilitated the Little Rock Bible Study as a support group since most of the members had their own ministries, as well. We relied on each other for encouragement and an occasional shoulder to lean on. Through this all, I still managed to do housework, raise the kids, work in my garden, sew, and receive the necessary training for the detention work. Oh, and I also carried food to terminal HIV patients who were confined to their homes, waiting to die. Nothing, however, was allowed to interfere with family life.

While in Santa Maria, among many dreams, I was in Heaven, walking in front of a house. I saw the Father, the Son and the Holy Spirit. This is just one of the many dreams and incidents recorded in my journals.

Holy Trinity; Father. Son and Holy Spirit

Finally at Santa Maria, Al became a retreat master, holding monthly weekend retreats. Right! More hospitality work for me, but we loved it! Then the Lord moved us to Texas.

———————————————

COMMENT FROM HER EULOGY: In Santa Maria CA at a time when no one else would get anywhere near them for fear of contagion (only later disproved), Jeannie carried food, solicitude and consolation to terminal AIDS patients, all at home awaiting on-rushing death. Yes, some even cried with joy, seeing Jeannie at their door.

She also taught CCD (Christian education) to teens and spent many hours and days visiting teenagers in detention; delivering communion, solicitude and consolation to all. At our departure from Santa Maria, the director of the detention center announced to his staff that Jeannie was the only volunteer staff ever (!), whom the kids in jail would ask for by name. When locked in their cells they would ask, "Is Mrs. Hughes going to come and see us?" They, and the AIDs patients, received the same charm, grace, humility, peace, charity, loving kindness and solicitude many came to know of her in these last years. She truly was the servant of all. But there is more.

JEANNIE'S TESTIMONY:
TEXAS LIFE

At Corpus Christi I got busy again, this time as the flower arranger for St Helena Parish. Didn't know much about flower arranging, so I hit the books and learned. With a couple of assistants we did do marvelous work, if I do say so, myself! Also, I perfected my quilting skills and turned out many a quilt as a prayer form, giving them away as the Spirit led.

During this time I had a dream of Kevin, who was miscarried in Fairbanks. I saw the Blessed Virgin Mary carrying a naked child.

Sometime later I wondered if she was carrying my son, Kevin. The dream shows he is in heaven. I ask him often to pray for his sisters, Shannon and Katie.

I also joined Birthright as my voluntary part of combating the evil of abortion. As this is being written, the last abortion clinic in town has closed. Thanks be to God. I used to stand on the sidewalk there, speaking to women who were about to have an abortion. Some changed their mind and walked away. Others ignored us or cursed us. Do they not know that our Heavenly Father knew our names before time began? That He has a plan for each of us? If they do not honor God and his plan for each child, who in Hell are they honoring?

And another thing. Same sex marriage and sexual relations also go against God's plan for us, as is the idea of women priests. There is no precedent for it and Mary, herself was not ordained. Saint John Paul II said during his pontificate that he had no authority to ordain women.

—————————•—————————

COMMENT FROM HER EULOGY: At Corpus Christi, she also served as St Helena sacristan and taught CCD for teens, while spending years at

Birthright, counseling young women on their duties to new life with the same charm, grace, humility, peace, charity, loving kindness and solicitude many have come to know of her in these last years. And still, there is more.

For twenty five years in CA and TX she was my right hand hospitality partner in our conduct of parish RCIA, retreats, and small faith community development. (RCIA is the "Rite of Christian Initiation for Adults.) And did I mention that in all this, over a 48 year span, she also managed to raise a husband from agnosticism to lay evangelist and raised two daughters as well? All this with the same charm, grace, humility, peace, charity, loving kindness and solicitude many have come to know in these last years. She truly was the servant of all. From the most notable to the most humble, she truly was the servant of all.

Jeannie's class quilt with each child's picture thereon.

JEANNIE'S TESTIMONY:
AND NOW...

I no longer can drive. My reflexes and reaction time are not what they once were. So far, my work at Birthright continues. Love still endures as my vocabulary diminishes; I tell you now, as taught by life and love in the Spirit, this I believe:

We all are accountable for our own actions in this life. The more I became involved in the life of others, the more I saw the need to respond to the deep pain I see in the lives of people I have met. I do not expect to make a great impact on the hurts that I see, but by being aware of them, I can respond with prayers of petition for our Lord to intercede. And the closer we get to the Lord, thereby, the more selfless we become.

I did have a profound spiritual experience while we lived in Antigua. It was charismatic, and over the years certain spiritual gifts have manifested themselves. I do experience prayer burdens. People will mention a concern and sometimes I feel compelled to pray, even fasting for a few days. Those prayers often are answered. Maybe a healing, maybe a conversion. God takes his own time: I prayed for Al eleven years before his conversion. I know that I must accept suffering for these prayer burdens. Recently, I have experienced increasing joy in that suffering. Usually the suffering comes in the form of isolation and being misunderstood by my peers and my siblings, though not by my husband. God routs out pride; He is creative in keeping me humble.

In the study of Scripture, I feel enlightened by certain passages, especially in the New Testament. Jesus really means what he says: He does not like luke-warm-ness. He wants us to follow Him whole heartedly in His Church. I see our Faith as a beacon on the shoreline, guiding us in rough seas, sure and steady, always there.

A FINAL COMMENT: Jeannie began a precipitous decline unto death six weeks before the end. We were at the Navy Exchange. I noticed that suddenly, like the snap of a twig, she could not talk, her walking became difficult, she seemed delirious, incoherent. She struggled over to the men's shoes and started looking. The salesman there was beside himself, trying to move her to the women's area. I took him aside, told him about the Alzheimer's and asked him to allow her whatever she chose. She selected an elegant pair of black men's shoes, which I paid for; and we departed. I thought no more of it.

After the funeral, finally alone at home, I noticed those shoes she had placed on a step stool under our bedroom window. I thought, "Poor dear, she was delirious." I left them there.

Perhaps a week later, I was standing before that same stool, staring at those shoes. Suddenly, I realized, she could not possibly have worn them! Then it dawned on me – she had not tried them on at the Exchange! I put them on. A perfect fit! In the midst of her final mental collapse, in her agony and confusion, she *still* was trying to serve. Those shoes, as gift, were her last mortal act of service!

The Monday before Jeannie's death on Saturday, 25 July, hospice ladies came by to describe their services and to unload on me a ton of government required paper work, all needing multiple signatures. But then, they began to ask about me; probing questions, getting somewhat personal. Finally, the leader gazed at me with a puzzled, worried look and asked, "Why do you seem so happy?"

I started with the text book answer, describing the benefits of detachment as opposed to the opposite which is co-dependence: That detachment is not an act of "not caring" (about Jeannie's pending death), but freedom from emotional involvement so that I was clear-headed and could make the best decisions whatever the situation. As professional social workers, they were educated in psychology; they understood, but were not satisfied. And so, I said, "Look. For 48 years, I have stood next to a living saint. What's not to like?" The three of them relaxed at that.

I then told them that, while watching Jeannie feed sea gulls at Port Aransas, our friend, Ken Justice, had named her "Saint Jeannie of Aransas."

This I did not, perhaps, should have, told them. As Jeannie's life was closing, we had met every commitment we had made to God in His expressed will; to our children in their care and education; and to one another in chaste, faithful, undying love. Furthermore, I had met my commitment to Ed Bond and to myself, while learning the true meaning of love by following behind the example of an orphan child, Gloria Jean "Jeannie" McCaffery Hughes; trying to mimic some measure of her charm, grace, humility, peace, charity, loving kindness and solicitude that all who ever met her came to know of her. She truly was the loving servant of all.

In the gospels it is written: *One who would be the greatest in the kingdom, shall be the servant of all.* These words, scripturally attributed to *Christos*, are the basis for our claim. Servant of all. That Jeannie lived, for that is who she is.

In the original first century sense of the word; as one authentically following Jesus, *Christos*, in His Universal (Catholic) Church; Jeannie certainly is a saint, qualified for – in Saint Paul's words – *the crown of justice.*

QED

QED is an abbreviation of the Latin "*Quod Erat Demonstrandum*" "that which was to be demonstrated." It is placed at the end of a mathematical proof to attest that the proof is complete.

POSTSCRIPT:

There are people who teach; neither by lecture, nor debate, nor by Socratic questioning, but by the conduct of their life. Jeannie was one such. Orphaned before her teens, from out of her loss of parental love and the intense loneliness of a child moved about, there came a new measure of love and care for the sufferings of others that is seldom seen. Such is the stuff of holiness. From such does a wounded healer emerge. Accomplished in league with Sacramental life, a holy Saint may be found.

All are called to holiness. If you are uncertain of the way, following Jeannie is a good start.

The shiny black shoes
of Saint Jeannie Hughes

THE HIGH CALLING

If God has called you to be really like Jesus in all of your life, he will draw you into a life of crucifixion and humility, and put on you such demands of obedience, that he will not allow you to follow other Christians, and in many ways He will seem to let other good people do things which He will not let you do.

Other Christians and ministers who seem very religious and useful may push themselves, pull wires, and work schemes to carry out their plans; but you cannot do it; and if you attempt it, you will meet with such failure and rebuke from the Lord has to make you sorely penitent.

Others can brag on themselves, on their work, on their success, on their writings, but the Holy Spirit will not allow you to do any such thing, and if you begin it, He will lead you into some deep mortification that will make you despise yourself and all your good works.

Others will be allowed to succeed in making great sums of money, or having a legacy left to them or in having luxuries, but God may supply you daily, because he wants you to have something far better than gold, and that is a helpless dependence on Him, that He may have the privilege of providing your needs day to day out of the unseen treasury.

The Lord may let others be honored, and put forward, and keep you hid away in obscurity, because he wants to produce some choice, fragrant fruit for His coming glory, which can only be produced in the shade.

God will let others be great, but keep you small. He will let others do a work for Him, and get the credit for it, but He will make you work and toil on without knowing how much you are doing; and then to make your work still more precious, He will let others get the credit for the work which you have done, and this will make your reward ten times greater when Jesus comes. The Holy Spirit will put a strict watch on you, with a jealous love, and will rebuke you for little words and feelings or for wasting your time, which other Christians never seem distressed over.

So make up your mind that God is an infinite Sovereign, and has a right to do as He pleases with His own, and He will not explain to you a thousand things which may puzzle your reason in His dealings with you. God will take you at your word; and make you absolutely sell yourself to be His slave. He will wrap you up in a jealous love, and let other people say and do many things that you cannot do or say. Settle it forever, that you are to deal directly with the Holy Spirit, and that He is to have the privilege of tying your tongue, or chaining your hand, or closing your eyes, in ways that others are not dealt with.

Now when you are so possessed with the living God that you are, in your secret heart, pleased and delighted over this peculiar, personal, private, jealous guardianship and management of the Holy Spirit over your life, you will have found the vestibule of heaven in Christ Jesus, our Lord.

Quoted from *JESUS IN EXODUS* by Michael Esses, p 245.

Abide with me; fast falls the eventide;
The darkness deepens; Lord, with me abide;
When other helpers fail and comforts flee,
Help of the helpless, oh, abide with me.

Swift to its close ebbs out life's little day;
Earth's joys grow dim, its glories pass away;
Change and decay in all around I see—
O Thou who changest not, abide with me.

I need Thy presence every passing hour;
What but Thy grace can foil the tempter's pow'r?
Who, like Thyself, my guide and stay can be?
Through cloud and sunshine, Lord, abide with me.

I fear no foe, with Thee at hand to bless;
Ills have no weight, and tears no bitterness;
Where is death's sting? Where, grave, thy victory?
I triumph still, if Thou abide with me.

Hold Thou Thy cross before my closing eyes;
Shine through the gloom and point me to the skies;
Heav'n's morning breaks, and earth's vain shadows flee;
In life, in death, O Lord, abide with me.

Henry F. Lyte